ONE AGE

in a

DREAM

One Age in a Dream

DIANE GLANCY

Illustration by
Jay Moon

Milkweed Editions

89 88 87 86   4 3 2 1

A LAKES & PRAIRIES AWARD BOOK
Published by *Milkweed Editions*
Post Office Box 3226
Traffic Station
Minneapolis, Minnesota 55403
Books may be ordered from the above address

Illustrated by Jay Moon © 1986

Library of Congress Cataloging-in-Publication Data

Glancy, Diane
    One Age in a Dream.

    Lakes and Prairies Award book

    I. Title.
PS3557.L29405 1986   811.54   86-62394
ISBN: 0-915943-20-4

This publication is supported in part by a grant
provided by the Metropolitan Regional Arts Council
from funds appropriated by the Minnesota State
Legislature, and by a grant from the National Endowment for the Arts.

Acknowledgment to *Cutbank* for "Evolution of the Sacred Dog" and
"Clothes Horse"; *Earth Chant* (Albuquerque, New Mexico) for "Let-
ter to My Father"; *Image Magazine* (St. Louis, Missouri) for "The In-
evitable"; *Midwest Quarterly* for "Sign Writer"; *Ironwood* for "Bride
Means Cook" and "Pasture for Rent"; *Croton Review* for "Right Justly"
and "Navajo"; *Wanbli Ho Journal* (Mission, S.D.) for "Second Hand";
Feminist Studies (University of Maryland) for "If Words Were Shapen
in the Animal Head" and "Squirrels"; *Puerto Del Sol* for "I Was" and
"Oyster Bed"; *Sunrust* for "Reparation."

For Joseph
who gave me time

ONE AGE IN A DREAM

Token

The Woodcarver

One Age in a Dream

ONE AGE IN A DREAM

Token

The whole is lost / & we are fragments of those wagons moving west. What shall I say of the land? Red man & white battered by heat & wind / the blizzards that sweep the prairie. We move through the rough terrain of circumstance / It may be the frontier no matter where we live. Character through hardship / The encouragement of pain. Yep. That's it.

The Inevitable

Strange how the long shadow in the family
photo points straight to her. The sun
coming down upon us in the farmyard like
a spotlight we try to get away from. But
not her, bold, grinning, standing out
from the group a bit, as though she is
not afraid of the black finger that seems
to pick her out.

See the wire in the corner of the picture,
my brother says, it is just the shadow of
a utility pole that makes a dark trough
across the bare yard to her.

Her eyes shine like ponds in the field—
her certainty that our lives sprout again
like new grass.

We look silently at the album.

I would like someone to talk to—perhaps
the gas station attendant who worked to
get bugs off our windshield after a trip
to the farm, the station sideways on the
corner—then we could lean out the window
and say to him—there's a chance our mother
is dying.

Stockton's Wing
on St. Patrick's Day with Dan

Something intrudes into the concert—
not as gay as the jig,
like the shirt you say you bought in Ireland
with no pockets
& someplace you stayed, a ghost pushed you
out of bed.

Stockton's Wing plays a song called,
                    Jenny's Chickens—
banjo, mandolin, fiddle,
a lively tinwhistle on tour.

The drummer waits then beats the drum
& talks to himself, he does,
winces like he plucked feathers
or ate gooseberries with a scowl,
saying bitter, bitter, but eating anyhow.

It is cold in Jenny's yard
& somewhere in the north country they play about
                    next—
There's a harshness they can't stomp out
with the strut of chicken's feet.

Sometimes children get the croup
& after a sling of nights
a door creaks open with a hand-made casket,
& a minister with raspy voice
says life is something to be endured.

The fiddle seems to smoke—
a backyard wood-fire
for washing sheets after the child is buried
& comes back on certain nights
to claim his bed.

The Drowned

Yonka Pioway
fields yellow in Kansas—
The haytruck sways
like a lone pond in the wind.
We could be children here
part of us remembers
the warped fields, the house bigger
than it is now.
The sun falling like a meteor
as though tossed by burning hands.

The night alone
we heard the chair move upstairs—
Still wonder
who sat in it when it scraped the floor?
The Indian girl who fished the pond?
Honkawah Ha.

The sparse house, these fields
furry with stubble.
The silos that dance the harsh
pulley with hay to the loft.
The rowboat rides the yellow skin
of the pond
bloated as squash.
Her arms & legs still reel
one more breath.

I Was

But am not Indian / no more

I picked a hole in the gourd
where stones fell out
backed over the turtle-shell-rattle / burst it flat

He yey

He hee / a woman in the bare yard
soaps the head of her retarded daughter /
the cat licks his paws
on the table by the butcher knife

I was Indian but am no more

Through with it

whRRRRRRR
my totem in the sawblade
little teeth crunch like rabbit leg
in coyote mouth

Then Butcher KNife in welder's helmet w/ warpaint
heats the metal teeth of the saw

He hee / we laugh

The woman in the yard pours water from a kettle
over her daughter's head
the girl squirms / Hold STILL
the mother said

Chonk A Wah

Old Indian woman
comesback to reservation
after blind school.
The bluing of her eyes like pale sunlight
in her head.
She holds the braille book on her lap,
moves her fingers along the slats of picket fence —
the gritty barnyard where white hens feed.
She lets us feel the raised holes
like shriveled pumpkins
or a colander pounded flat
with little eyelets for the rain she absorbs
upthrough the roots of her fingers —
her stems —
rising to the blue suns of her head.

Looking for a Word I Can't Spell

A radiator for my birthday!

Boaz, I take what you leave
in the border of the field.
Earlier it was tires, brakes,
a heater when it was cold.

Now this lovely radiator with shiny,
corrugated sides —
a large, black briefcase
slipped into the front of the car
like a compact into a purse.

I can't go without it
over meadows
where little barns pop up along the road
and streams run like a hose.

Oyster Bed

The fourth grade boy brings me his journal
when I come to talk about poetry.
I've seen these blank books
in dimestores
with blue waltz perfume, oil cloth,
and garters.

I turn the pages
knowing I draw out something hidden —
old boundaries along a shifting river
where Oklahoma, for instance, drifts into
Texas or Arkansas
and sometimes back again.
We always hear about it here,
and how it takes a court battle
to decide the state in which a man's acreage lies.

It is as though the fourth grade boy
pries open a shell,
his blunt knife stuck into the crack and turned
until the slit opens
like a wound stuck shut with moss and spit.

What do you write about? He asks.

Whatever I can, I answer.
He smiles and I see the swirl of his ears
like two halves
of an oyster shell.

His gray pencil-marks
eddy the unlined dimestore journal.
Sometimes these books are titled —
"Points of Interest in Kansas"
or something to let you know there is not much
to notice in this world
where he brings me these pages he writes,
these pearls.

Opposed

Pieces of houses over a tract / cleared land for other houses far into the country / I used to sow these pastures in my head / Nights join days with a kitchen leg, another child's room with a hole for a doorknob like an esophagus / Broken window-box out of which other boxes bloom & from them begonias, geraniums / a woman sitting on her backporch, hands gripping her knees. How can they plow under the land for more houses? Where are field grass & white chickens supposed to go? Shunned as a woman with a sickness or with a child no one wants to claim.

Reparation

All morning I wait at the east window
where fields smother the root cellars
& sod houses covered a hundred years.
I hang up your clothes, son,
walk down the hall.
Soon they wheel you back on a gurney
tinkling like a liniment peddler
& you are in the room with me again.
I gave you up so you could be returned.
Your breathing stretches
through the night.
The first light breaks & these coarse
trees shoot a hundred arrows upward
as though from an Indian raid.
You turn in bed & moan.
A campfire burns in your side
where the doctor pushed muscle back
into place & sewed up your gap.
You will mend—
Threads of prairie grass close
the drought-cracked soil. On the hori-
zon, the fence, even, stitches field to
sky, though they keep tearing in the
groin, like you.
Out here, we still make wild at-
tempts to hold our things together.

Easter Morn

This emptiness is not the emptiness
when they came to the tomb & he
was gone.
That emptiness had possibility.
Even the thought his body was taken
gave them something.
But this emptiness
draws everything into it
like the hole in the front yard
my father-in-law poured dirt into thirty years
& after his death
his widow still carries dirt to it.
Not everyday, you understand,
& not a large hole —
Sometimes she keeps a brick over it.
Then it sinks
until you think of a crater in the moon.
It must be an underground well
or a cave, or cellar —
Someone insists on opening the door
& everything falls in.
You know the kind of windy day
that blows papers across the room.

It makes you swoon to think of the yard
sinking a little all the time
even during sleep —
And you wonder what foundation
reality holds.

Just look in court rooms at cratered families.
You feel the emptiness that swallows bricks.
You wound & deceive.
You cannot get along —
 Look at caves which pull you in like animals
that hibernate in darkness.

Think of the way it feels when you argue
with the man you married twenty years ago
& still might love because it hurts
to see him suffer but you need money & he needs it
& you fight one another
until grief pulls you into itself.
You gnaw on the other's limbs
as though they were stalks of corn in a field
where someone struggled against drought
& maybe dug this well that sinks in the yard,
though you can't be sure of anything
except emptiness.

Somewhere in the earth
dirt from my father's-in-law bucket
& bricks my mother-in-law covered the hole with
fall like young girls into craters
appeasing gods
& you wish for something to soothe your anger.

You feel the hole in yourself
& in your pocket—
The struggle for goods when there isn't enough
and he has most of it—

Sometimes anger spouts like old volcanoes
& sparks fly up into a larger realm.
Things are different there—
Something more than squabbling on the earth.
You become enlarged.
What will it matter in a hundred years?

But now it is painful—
this hole in which your guilt & rage
& sympathies are drawn when you see his writing—
the awkward letters like someone screaming.

Perhaps in this tomb on Easter morning
emptiness is no more hollow than the hope
on which your foundation rests,
& possibility holds you like gravity
that makes a slight dent in the yard
over which you stand with your brick.

How

Sleeping Face & Old Bull Thigh,
a row of beaver bones for a rib-
vest, a canoe-shaped smile, sit
in the shade & say the ancestors
came to the new world bobbing
under sealskin floats on the land-
bridge under the Bering Straits.
They hunted mammoths, planted
maize & beans & squash & the sky
seemed clear was soon crammed
with clouds, every corner of it,
like settlers' wagons & then
farmers' sheds built with scraps
& stuffed with cultivators & hay
& the dust storm with lightning
sparklers rolled up the prairie
with its night & how swatting flies
the ancestors must have wondered
what land bridge the white man
crossed, what mammoth he followed
from the other way.

Over blue pines

flamingos and a herd of coyotes.

Thistles by the road wave like little hands of children.

Corridors into the wilderness where the flamingos graze
and cabin roofs slope with pines.

What passes in the sky tonight?

Scabby ghosts hovering near old battle grounds—

Tiger Butter

Is it only when you're little
you know tigers live in your closet—
one with your shoes on his two ears,
another with your umbrella tied to his tail;
the rest wearing your red coat
and blue trousers with the red buttons?
Is it only when you're little
the dustballs have mountainous shadows
in the crack of light under the door?
Or is it also NOW you fear that tigers will eat you—
when you wake in the middle of the night
and don't know where you are,
nor remember how far you've come.
Your nose hurts like a plowed field,
your fingers stiff—
Then somehow, you remember what you've accomplished.
The sewing is finished—
The red buttons threaded to the blue pants
and the little coat with its sleeves.
And you know you have given them to the tigers
(so they won't eat you).
But they chased themselves around a tree
and melted into butter.
NOW you can pick up your coat and trousers,
your shoes and umbrella.
Soon, even, you can start your car and go—
The promise of dawn already
on the face
of the clock-radio.

Pasture for Rent

I would rent the pasture
if I had horses,
their hooves like wind
through new grass,
barefoot as guests
at a wedding
after dancing all night.
But dawn washes in
with sobering light
& I remember how the husband
lifted his bride's veil
to wipe her eyes.
What did she cry about
as she danced
with her new husband,
her father & brothers,
heart thundering
like horses in her chest?
Is she like the squirrel
who starts across the road
then suddenly, half-way,
turns back?
Just wait
until she is an old woman
with a string
pinned to her zipper
to pull it up the back
of her dress.
Then she will have reason
to cry into the emptiness
of the pasture for rent.

Token

Greeting the Transition

Winter departs like relatives
who stay too long —
but even when they leave
there are things left —
some recipes she gave them,
perhaps a potted plant on the sill,
a box of wool clothes they'll come back for.
Then it will be spring —
the earth soft as dough for gingerbread,
the afternoon hot as an oven.

I know she often thought
nothing would get done because of me.
Her words black as china tea when I looked at her
from my knee-hole desk.

Mother, how many times I sit
at the table wondering why
I didn't open the book to read
until others were nearly through.
I didn't tie back
the honeysuckle
but let it spill over the gate —
I didn't inflate the speckled
rubber fish
but left it flat
as this butter knife
against the plate.

Bride Means Cook

PHILADELPHIA—*That word
"bride" comes from an old Teu-
tonic word meaning "to cook."*

Now there are bean poles
in the small field by the house,
trellises waiting to be climbed.

Now the raw, barely green wife
comes from the door,
her club feet,
her spiny fingers push seed
like hard bird droppings into the ground.

Give them a few warm days,
let the sun provoke the seeds.

Let the man know what to do with his wife—
how to take her soft, wet stalk
into his fingers,
make it grope for the light
with asparagus and bean sprouts—

Let her climb her new name
and cover the field with her pods.

Let her soak in a jar of water
and rise like pintos in a boiling pot.

Letter to my Father

Maybe your grave on a hill much like this one
brings you back more
than on other Father's Days.

I climb the slope,
look at the city in the distance,
just as another city stands in view from your
cemetery.

The buildings are tall as granary silos
beside railroad tracks
when we used to go to grandfather's farm.

You were a quiet man, gave me an Indian's sense
of land.
The summer already a cauldron,
you touch my face with the rising heat.
When blowing grass brushes my legs
I remember your ways.

You could wear the same shirt until mother
told you to take it off.
Her complaints moved slowly as the open mouths
of barn doors from the road.

I am still on the farm.
The wild turnips I pull are small white clouds
with roots of heat-lightning in the distance.

I pick a cornflower on the hill,
feel the stamen beneath its soft petals
and remember your arm I touched at the end.

I wave the flower like a mourner
with a tiny blue handkerchief.
Your steadfastness holds me
when I want to fall off the hemisphere of
the hill
and city is nothing more than quavering silos
in the sun.

Prior to the Heart

The day of my grandparents' accident
our yard seemed high
I must have been eleven when they drove
from the farm
Some boys coming from the other way
didn't stop at the crossroads
Rammed them like my brother at the bedroom door
angry that I took off the knob
and stood against it
so he couldn't push through like the floor-shift
into my grandfather

We stayed with the woman next door
when they called my mother
Rid of us for once
she went to the farm
I watched my father mark the end of the garden
while she was gone
a fat, hard beetle strummed the air with his legs
helpless as grandpa
near fields of grazing cattle
up under the sun

The blue sky with white clouds like lambs
on the calico dress my grandmother made
Not the sweet English pastures
of her grandparents'
But out here on this harsh prairie
I don't turn over the beetle
Let him struggle where the end of the row
is marked

Old Prairie House Between Tulsa and Bartlesville on US 75

I

Back in time
car in yard
shutters at windows
paint on gray boards
old man, old woman
their children gone
then man and woman younger
        with young children
west wing not yet built on house
one wagon, horse arrive
untended land
back too far
young man, woman with eyes
        like bright baubles
holding space
one shutter closes on another.

II

Grizzled, unpossessed
on the ledge of plains
factional roof
meager walls written upon
like points of long prairie grass
the house stares across the highway
as though remembering a fir tree
        carried on horseback
through blinding snow.

III

Survival of facade
when content does not endure
one part has nothing to do with the others
all is hollow
ramshackled
but house still stands on prairie
customs still leap on points
        of delicate prairie grass
where the bright bauble of the eye
blinked once too often.

I Hear Your Jive

You comb your hair straight up
and it stays —
Bleached ripe as a field.
Who knew you would look like
a head of wheat?
Emulator of grain —
your punk generation is aware
of hunger.

1945/1985

My cat suns herself in our little yard this morning
she brings back memories of the house where I was born
while mother wrote to my uncle overseas
I sat in my bonnet & sunsuit among flowers
half the world was torn by war
the vineyards in france the gardens in germany
& england

the scorched stationary of japan

now in a battle zone of my own
I think of those places holding their little postage-
stamps of peace

Walls of the School White as Milk

In the shade in back of the school
no grass grows.
The children take their books & lunch boxes
into the building while birds peel back
their sound.
I look again for the earrings
I know I lost—
delicate filigree.
I had them in my bag and they ran.
Not like birds
nor children
but silently
as buffalo who wandered in prairie grass for years
now shrunken like heads in a museum—
they belong with those things
which can never be replaced.

Bangladesh

The trouble is the land is flat & at
sea-level. A tidal wave can wash in
after any cyclone like a hand sweeping
a table, clearing it of everything.
Rice fields, bamboo houses, a few grass
mattresses, families, swept out to sea.
Some probably still asleep. The air
knocked out of them before they woke,
gulping as though lungs hungered for
water, knee-deep in it most everyday.
The children just born shuttered any-
way from air above rice fields &
grass roofs of the huts, now their lit-
tle hands wave gentle again as seaweed.

Little Beaver

Head bent forward almost on her chest.
Quilted poncho,
muzzle of polka dots.

She wears a wolf mask & looks fierce
as she sweeps the piled-stick mound—
Paints a raccoon tail on her flat brown one.

Man with hoedown head
fiddlestrings the fields.

Covered wagons like a row of opossum,
a swarm of cars like beetles.

Tomatoes allemande with mulberries
while the man sings with blue electric rings
around his eyes.

Later the trolley moving all over town
but only on its tracks.

We say to her,
it's all right.

What children she has gathered about her,
what spirits with open wombs.

Black Mesa
(El. 4,978 feet, Highest Point in Oklahoma)

Open range,
cows cross the road in front of us.
Land flat as the kitchen floor
with squares of shrub pines for tiles.

When we stop
the wind shovels
the undercurrent of birds—
twitters & buzzers
with a code of their own making.

We take the umbilical cord of a small road
north from Kenton.

The mesa,
a kitchen table when I was eye-level to it.
Pillars of rock
like salt & pepper,
vinegar castor.

Sage brush, telephone poles.

One rock formation open
as the mouth of a bass papa caught.

The Stone Marker

I lift it in the car quickly
before a thought of leaving it occurs—

A petrified loaf of bread
        a flat step into a stone line-camp shed
where cowboys gravitated on long trips
to the range—

Maybe a territorial marker
or headstone carved by a squatter?

No, it is a stone baby just born—
a notch at the top for a face.

I coddle it a moment thinking
        land run, dust bowl, now these green fields
like a play pen
or a crib for new crops.

Wheeless, Oklahoma, 7 Miles

We drive further than that
and never find it.

Patches of plowed-up land
like an old trunk
from which black rollers with static electricity
still rise.

Hay rolls seem dustballs on this attic floor
between Texas & Colorado
almost to New Mexico.

The oil pumper grazes up & down
with a lean horse in the field.

Grain elevators are toilet-paper tubes
lined up to make rocket ships.

We pass a blindfolded house,
the shed boarded also in this attic crawl space—
this launching pad
through which the wide sky waits.

Picture in a Museum:
Squatters on No Man's Land
(The Oklahoma Panhandle)

Their faces are quite open
though one scowls.

Maybe somewhere within them
they dance like clothes on the line —
their heart a kind of a shed
for mules that pulled the wagon.

Kind of disheartening —
their place on the raw plains.
Maybe they don't know.

Their stamina coarse as the collar
that grips their neck.

They hover near the sod walls
of their house in No Man's Land —
a cow & some chickens,
inside
two mattresses & a roughhewn table & chairs.

Over them the blue sky,
a sagging cloud,
a bird rising bleached as a skull.

For my Daughter on Memorial Weekend

I should have asked how you felt
with the holiday on your hands
like an empty room to fill.

I never had enough of myself to give.
You always drew on resources I didn't have—
eager to escape my hollowness,
I grew smaller all the time.

Down to nothing & into nothing—
the great universe of it
grows larger all the time.
It is itself an entity with something to give—
the barrenness of the land.
Black Sunday when the first cloud passed
in the dust bowl.

You have told me how you felt—
Your anger that your father & I left the family
in shambles—
You & your brother have a harder time
than if we had stuck it out like dirt storms.

You are without support of family.
Possibly you already know the nothing within.
I felt it with my mother—
not able to say what I needed to—
I still hold the words within me like a cluster
of shriveled children
not born.

I hate to leave,
but the long weekend is a room I must fill—
a hollowness that carries weight.

At night in our separate beds,
the elements pass over us as they are—
sparkling with great, dark mystery
& these little wonderments of despair.

The Woodcarver

Perseus in Arkansas

Well, jipes! I floored the Chevy/
fishtailed all over the soft-tarred
road

Old women babbling by the church
shit no one with balls
goes to flea markets

the road festered at Pelsor
curves at sixty-two

overturned once on these roads
still don't know how I got out.

The Mothers Speak

1. ADRIENNE TALKS ABOUT THE APPLE ON THE TABLE

One child and I am no longer my own.
He is the apple
the table and chair.
I inherit his bleak land
to fill with tree and cloud
and car on the distant road in the woodgrain
of the table.
I harvest fields as salvage
for the hollow land he sets within.
Trees hit the car.
I would go back,
travel without hindrance,
but I would only birth a distant flock of birds
tiny as a baby's head.

2. THE MOTHER OF PERSEUS

For years I floated in a wooden box
my father had the woodcarver make for my son and me.
It's a fear of his that his grandson will kill him.
Silly.
Men, you know.
Irrational at times.
But he always was distant.
He used to take me to the games in Argos
but I think it was to show me I was not his son.
I could have been a boy.
I was thin with cropped hair.
Even when I see myself now I am amazed at my thinness.
I thought the birth of my son
would reconcile us
but it spooked him and we've lived in exile
all these years.

Jewks, the Woodcarver

I carve wooden Indians, scarecrows, dolls and strings,
a cane from the branch of a hedge-apple tree.

A box for a man in Argos.

Church pews, wooden organ pipes.
Christmas trees.

Candles.
Wooden apples.   Eggs.   Teeth.   porra   porra   wurrrrrrr

Wood cow and horse.
Headstone.

I carve light running out of the hedge-apple tree,
mimic its dance in wax
down the candleside.

Kato

I watch Jewks carve from the orange trumpet creeper.
His gray hair, a low halo on his head. At times,
I sweep his woodshavings. Sometimes, he carves our
wooden meals. Behind the mill, the sawdust piles up
like mounds of haystacks, but his leavings curl like
sheep wool. His hands shake gently as he works
and the hair at the back of his head saw-tooths from
sweat.

Wig Maker

We're amazed at the bald Medusa
when her snakes hunt in the barnyard.
Later they return with chicken eggs lodged in their bellies.
Then she is spangled—
as though under boughs hung with glass balls
in the glorious season.

She tells us she is having a wig made:
snakes carved from wood,
more reliable, less likely to leave,
a farmwife with nowhere to go.

The shed leans as though sat on while she talks
on her run-down place.
Already bored, we regret the visit.

The twisting mass of hair reminds us of the exchange
of interstates
where blue prairie unfolds like a map.

She says she worries about Perseus,
a beanied garage mechanic in the small town,
his winged sandals and cap, grease rag.

We stand on one foot then the other.
She reminds us of the chance of a severed head.

Brush along the river still pushes us like a regiment.
Orange flowers we've never asked the name of
jump in the yard.

She goes on about her troubles
and we can do nothing about them.

Our braids firm as snakes,
hands in our pockets, we look up the road,
waiting for gravel to lift like dust behind our truck.

We listen with indifference to Medusa,
hardened by these visits to her place,
our eyes already on the highway to a bigger town.

Ey, Jewks,

Maybe was in California once, carved haystacks out of
yellow hills, dreams not realized stronger than ones
that dance in viney orchards like berry stains on a
shirt. Between these hills, dreams pile up like grain.
Cantaloupe, yellow melon seeds: wild buttons on a vest.

But now I'm in the hills of Arkansas. I make my liv-
ing by carving what people want. A wooden chest. Raf-
fle ticket. Hymnals. I live alone. I work in the
mornings under the heavy trees that ring in the yard.
Traffic passes on the backroad. Cars stop now and then,
but people irritate me. They always need something.
Wood hub-caps for the wall of the gas station. Old bot-
tlecaps. That damned Perseus again! And Medusa, my
sister. I'm carving wood snakes for her hair. The
crosshatching on their scales is difficult—I've cut
myself several times. Snakes are not
easy. She should be satisfied with what she's got. But
no one is. That's why I carve until the evening sky
turns pinkish-orange as gasoline.

In these hills, the world is whacked off like unneeded
pieces on a carving. They should make us forget our
longing, but some use them "for getting" what they don't
have. A wooden horse for Epsey when she was little, a
wooden bottle for her milk. I wonder at times if they
are real or only out of my head in these isolated hills.
I may have carved my own head and out of it comes the
other carvings. A wood church. Pipe organ. These
hills are to be reckoned with. Post oaks. Ponds that
float flat on sloping hills. Goats in the yards. Wood
piles. A car that doesn't run. Wheejeebay. The an-
cestors speak with wooden tongues. Indians crossed
these hills from the east. Oliver Horse did not stop
but went on to California. The yellow hills/ piles of

grain/ he wrote back /our dreams fulfilled. Ee bow jabe.
Light filters through the trees. I want wooden ears not
to hear it all. I have to hire an apprentice soon if
Kato won't stay. Some of the yellow hills are not smooth
but have tire marks like snakes. Someone with smaller
hands to do some of the fine carving. Night rips the
screens and makes light run out at the end of the day.
These hills comfort a man. In the garden, wooden corn is
up. I dig for night crawlers and red worms under the
wooden squeak of limbs. These hills, fields, need to be
saved.

Letters

You and your several cats can come / Kato/
el gato, el gato, y los gatos /
my dog and I would welcome you / warmly, Jewks

Dear Jewks,
I have to stay at my house and fold the clothes
I washed and I am working on a small door
for my cats.

Kato

Dear Kato (y gatos)

What comfort in your blue house with half-folded
linens / halved peaches shriveled to the core /
your several cats.

I only can imagine you with a string around your
neck to hold your glasses to your chest / tie
your world there / by the heart you give to cats.

I admire your inventiveness and the maintenance
of your inventions.

But your answers / Kato / are not as true as the
problems.

Warmly,
the woodcarver, Jewks

The Three Sisters Flea Market

They have one eye between them
which they take turns with,
each removing it from her forehead
when she has it for a while
and handing it to another.

They have one chair between them,
which they exchange the same way,

and one cane.

Not all of them together
at one time can see, sit and walk.

But when two are blind
the third one sees the table we are looking at,
our own eyes half closed
to understanding

and when one is walking with us through the junk, the
piles and piles of it they keep in their flea market,
the one who sees tells the one who walks
which way we turn.
The cane tapping gently
gently at our side.

And the one who sits
waits for the others to finish,
wondering if she will first see
or walk
or maybe desiring neither but only the state of rest
in which she dwells,
not walking,
not seeing the catastrophe of the flea market:
wampum belt, wooden fish on a pole, yellow root,
the moon with war paint on its face, the smell of time,
peach stones, Indian chants, wee hee ya tey, sacred ground
in a jar, peace pipe, coral, twine, a sign, *Pray Jesus
Comming*, from a church somewhere in the hills, a bed, a
chest of drawers, wooden barrel, snake cage

some junk
never sold
but waits for an eye to see it,
a cane to tap it,
the foot to take it from the store.

The Woodcarver

Epsey

Wicked stepmother
witch worse than fathers'
first wife he married
mother to us first
witch woman
horse face in these hills
takes father's house
the first wife left
takes it all herself
why should children
suffer for what the wicked
wife did?
She didn't love the father
went to another man
second wife came
with her own child
pulls out the hair of our
head she takes bed and
chest whoopoo
the Star of Bethlehem quilt
the trout with the river
still around it.
She says it's hers and his
her chilern well
she's a mean woman
wants it all herself
whoop whoop
on thur backporch playing
the cords of her meanful
disposition.
The outhouse takes it all
and never gives back nuffum
but the stench of her.
For our chrismas tree
we have corn tassels for tinsel

and strings that tied up the
beans.
She is sour as a new apple
a horse tail stickin
out of her skirt.
Her hooves clap the porch
she is her own appreciation
with the scrawling brat
we sit under the step whee whee
doozin nuthin but et mud
our little snouts
cubbered with scabbers
from eatum nuffum but mud
while she has the feathered fan
the corn yellow hair
the wooden horse teeth.

Dear Kato

Carving is not enough. We have cup, plates,
knife, jamjar, cupboard, sinkboard, night
crawlers, brown trout rusted as the tin roof
of a shed,

buttons, melon, quilt, pillow, a window thin
and blue as milk. The witness of the earth's
curve on the moon.

But carving is not enough! There must be
utterance and even then / Kato / utterance
may not be enough!

                    Jewks

Kato (1) Talks to Adrienne

Well, he asked me to move into his house
with my awkward table and tribe of cats.

Jewks! the woodcarver. And I did!

Even Geronimo w/ hairpin whiskers when he jumped
on the woodstove.

Now Jewks is angry and takes it out on me.

We have the cup / he says / where is the tea?
We have a hog / where is the smokehouse to cure it?

I have the afternoon whitewashed in the sun.
Where is purpose?

You make the needs of people / I say.

Hang the people. He carves a noose.
Where is the smoke? The fire? The cured ham?

Only these cold, volcanic pits of peaches on the table.

Kato (2) Talks to Jewks

You asked me to be your apprentice. To sweep
your woodshavings and to carve some lines for you–

We have our community together.
It is not small and insignificant to me!

But why do you feel restless?
I sweep the woodshavings. That's the most I can do
for you now. Keep them from filling your small head.

I wished the questions changed as quickly as the answers/
you say.

I stand with you / Jewks / and forgive your gouges.
Now be quiet & carve your fields throbbing with grain.

It Used to Take Days

It was easier to stop
when we didn't drive so fast
through these hills.

Back then,
we could see the roadside stands
of apples and quilts
long before we got there.

Now we're past a place
before we know we want to stop.

It seems that everyone has gone.
Cemeteries are larger than the towns.

If we walked through these stony fields
we would find skeletons of rabbits
and squirrels,
smell the woodsmoke from old stoves
and hear porches swept with cornhusk brooms.

Now cars whizz past from the other way
like games in a video parlor.
Their streaks of yellow light remind us
of goldenrod we gathered for graves
of relatives
we hardly remembered
but were supposed to mourn.

If we stopped,
the past might swallow us
like corn relish and muscadine preserves.
Clothes hung up to dry
have sleeves
like mouths of open graves.

It used to take days to get through these hills.
Now we flash past
the rag man on a rusted bicycle
and startle a flock of crows that veil
the sky
with widow's lace.

To Squirrels, Who Wants to Marry His First Cousin

I always say look at the flea market sisters if you want
sumthun like them fer your children then marry Epsey.

What the Jewks!
Yeu doen weren't that darn n'uther in the awfulest jamber.

You can wait, Squirrels.
Duen't nothum n' serch a hurry.

Numphp.

Let me tell you what gumption is, Jewks says,
it's knowing you don't have nothum you can do
and duin it anywise.

For the Marionette I Had as a Girl (Epsey)

She moves with erkwerd feet.
When her jaw opuns, mule-teeth show.
There is no thoughts
in her wooden head.
Nothin comes together, sparks far*
in her solid mind.
Her nose ders not even grow with lies
if she could talk
Pinocchio-like.
Iders n'ert cross her mind with a flash
that draws an enward glance like mine.
She knows no transgression ner duesn't repent.
She has hair like chocolate surfflé.
Gaudy in her tafferta plaid dress and camisole,
she looks at me with leathery eyes.
Her gangly arms crawl
spider-like in air.
She dangles from wires in shiny black shoes,
her smile frightful
as the lacquered almonds on her round cheeks.
She is the dancing gypsy woman
harrowing my memory with her tambourine.

*fire

If Words Were Shapen in the Animal Head

I would speak these boreholes
in the shut room where myself the animal lives
but duersn't speak.

Leaves fall like comets,
wood shavings curl their fangs.

I jump back with claw.
Enow. Bark. Bark.

E jam sisss. Bark.

The rain smell jibbers my nose
flogs my head
scents wettened shoot up noseholes with jabs.

Open ground its smells run out like a stepped
on ant hill. Ignites thur fire.
Smoke sucks back a blue white eerie hole.

Ee bot aygo.

She-who-gives-food and he-who-carves
is not the man who used to kick.

Foots of man kicking tail between my legs.
Cur.
Black bejabbers my head
nothing
he kick kick
the gnaw in my rib black knife sharpen my ass.

Oblossom on twigs.
Er ghoot.
He callen me come to be hit legs given
under knife gone into tail
tied to post hit hit the boreholes
my head blue fire legs quiver black.

Scureb says the dog kick in howls
falls tooth like stars

but her-with-cats
and man-who-carves shavings blossom on his
wood piles.

Squirrels

Things come slower to us in Arkansas. Has to get
through these hills and we don't know n'uther way fer
them to get here but wait.

Fer it t'come knowden them comin from elsewhere.

But nuth dah other it weren't for nothin we wait
callin from ther door to hear iffen they ansared yit.

We know'd sometimes too we seein it as it donned
survived but we don't seeing it like it is
we knows lots going on round us we don't even see
it makes us feel blind/deef.

Can't know nothin anywise or ifen we see and knowd
somefin
we goes through it so fast we dun't know what ert wuz.

We sawin and Jewks says we loosin it even before we gebt.
Nurthin werz it any wize.

He whee
bay toh
eh eh
bay toh

All morning we saw   the old truck in two.

It teeters a moment, convulses and falls.

The bed for a trailer   the cab, a chicken coop.

The callous of a fallen shed   on the finger of land.

We sawin he-he the old truck all day finally it fallen
en' 2 like old sick dog been beaten.

Garage Mechanic's Lament

Was driving my truck down the road didn't know ennie
body else driving would be there just riding bushes
flapping past like a covey when you shoot into it
trying to be faster on the road than Squirrels had no
idea he would be there all uf a sudden hit his truck
in the crossroads killed him flat. Mother screaming
it were my grandfather I killed. I didn't know. We
all have to go. Zib woo.
Fill er up or grease yeur plugs?

Thurn I killed the old woman her no reason nuther than she
were a crazy hag and had ner reason ter live and took
her when she didn't know I was there hardly knew it myself.
How does these things happen in the hills?
We have choice dun't we? I ask.

Nuh, we dun't. Squirrels says.
Jurs driving on the road trying to go faster to go no-
where and t'othurs jes ther in our way.
Can't help it nothing no we can't.

Killern her when she jumped up on ther old hag humpin
her quick an her haid clean cut off 'ir neck.

Jewks Talks to Kato and Adrienne (About Her Sister's Son)

Bring me Epsey's tool to sharpen with the stone.
She whacks at branches
leaves them with blunt ends (crying over Perseus).

Chisel, gouge, rasp, file.

My tool shed (a blue wedge of sky between the hills).

They still dig up pieces of moccasins and blankets
they say belonged to Indians who crossed northwest
Arkansas on their removal trail to Indian Territory.

A red woman dances in yellow socks with snakes in her
hair.
She was my sister, Adrienne, though we weren't close.

The sun a tool I sharpen on the wedge of trees (the
growl of clouds cross the old road of the sun).

Perseus' Mother at the Trial

My Perseus not having a chance at school /
we moving continually

and all the humping:
bulls on cows
like ocean waves   rushing at the shore
when we were in the wooden box.

He is a youth and has been for years /
finally overcomes the reason in his head /
kills one by accident

and the other /
her always moaning in the outhouse
til she lets go of it like a lover

drives me knuts too

the past tight on us as an Indian head-band.

Now he rescues one from despair /
the girl he took from her mean father

He don't mean evil /
his rod and staff   a comfort to me.

Quiet as the Courthouse when Perseus Gets Acquitted

A longing for the plum orchard
that used to be,
the green sky now a quilt over us
instead of leaves.

For a while,
the orchard was only old,
but one by one
the branches left,
some in wind, some by ice,
now the trunks point to all that is over us,
in the sky.

On being once in Oklahoma during
the dust bowl
Oliver Horse said streets so silent he heard the click
when lights changed
and then dust blurred the red, the green,
the plums of our dark heads.

Perseus Marries a Girl
He Rescued from an Abusive Father
(Jewks and Kato Attend the Wedding)

A thicket of bittersweet by the fencerail /
twigs
brown-rust /
bent to the brown hills broken with wild yellow oats.
Your eyes are chicken coops, Perseus.
White hens clucking.
On the hill the breed of black angus
with the white band around their middle:
a wedding veil
while snow falls in cornrows /
the first bits of it/rice after your wedding.

Kato Says to Jewks,

You say you search for transition / but carve wood.
You stay with your forms / relationships of those forms.

You are a constellation / like him /
but I fall into space as a loose star.

Now you are revolutionary, Jewks, to forgive /
while I am glued to this house with anger.

The Young Wife of Perseus Speaks

Quilts hang like bibs on the line. The sky is
new cotton, stiff, not yet faded nor stained,
blue with a small print of white clouds. The
wind turns pages of a child's book, dried paste
in the edges of the binding like small, transparent
spider eggs. Mexican Star, Catch Me If You Can,
quilts with barbed-wire borders. A crib for
Electryon.

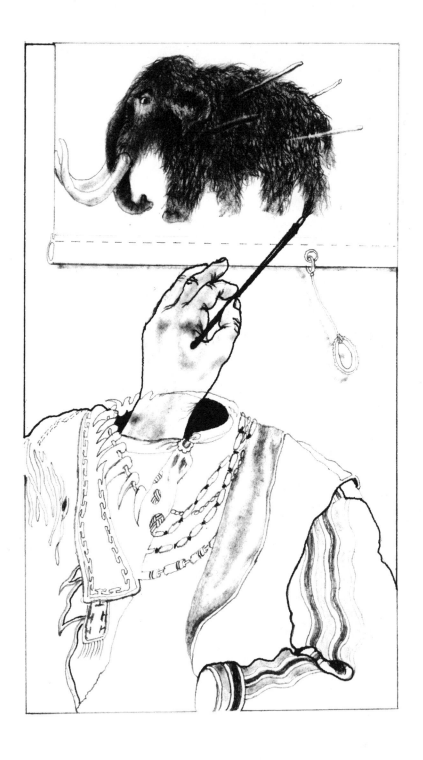

One Age in a Dream

For Ha-Pah-Shu-Tse (Red Corn) & Arbogast

who the first time they heard poetry said what is it?
She has holes in her head and just jumps in the holes
That's all she does

Her wild feet scatter across the yard
She never could run a straight line

Oh no

Poetry does not always follow a sense of logic
No it
leaps like a grasshopper on this dry ground

You just try and follow in bare feet
when the brittle grass reaches near September

& you'll see why the hops

Douglas Mail Plane

I make his bed one morning,
catch a corner
with the blanket I shake
with a whack,
bring down the Douglas Mail Plane
he glued together.
All night my son dreams
under these planes.
Not just across the blank prairie
but flying somehow
from the last realm into the next.
Out here we are just discovering
that we are.
Our engines revved.
Our words sent up as flares.

The Sign Writer

(A Painting in Gilcrease Museum, Tulsa, by Olaf Carl Seltzer)

The sign writer squats
on the rump of his horse
where buttes rise from the land.
He paints horses, the tracks of horses,
and a sun holding up its fingers
on the wall of the rock.
His signs are for the tribe that follows,
pointing to water and food
several days ahead.
The writer scratches his signs
with buffalo gallstones,
tints them with clay
moistened from glands
and the eyes of buffalo.
Oh chee ay. Oh chee.
His signs splint the fissures in the rock.
His signs spread ointment from his moving hand.

Osage County Museum, Pawhuska, Oklahoma

It's mostly the same here
slow as melonvines in an arctic sun
where the great ball of the plane
went down in nineteen thirty-five & an eskimo
with a camera took a picture that stayed
in his camera twenty-one years
& by some chance he told
an explorer who bought the film
& found the crash
& the bodies under tarp looking like
two seals on the ice,
the crumpled plane with oversized pontoons,
the propeller as though
it could turn again—
the men, Wiley Post & Will Rogers,
still twelve miles southwest of Barrow, Alaska.

Second Hand

You tell me the lame elk
paws the snow
outside your cabin
again this winter.
The others wait
while he nuzzles
the smothered grasses.
He defends his plot of ground
when they come near,
snorting,
butting with his head.

He eats close to the window
while you watch.
Maybe so you will see
his struggle,
his bravery & valiance.
Maybe this is the lesson
he holds out to you,
as though you were tame enough
to eat from his hand.

Evolution of the Sacred Dog

Our fathers called the horse
sacred dog

tied crow feathers to his mane

four trunks of legs
our fathers rode,

Now
afraid-to-fly
in grandfather clouds

our eyes
shrivel to walnuts

we tie crow feathers to our seat
tell ourselves
the plane is sacred horse.

Clothes Horse

Heifer brown in her buckskin dress
Horse in corral
with sun across its mane brown

Falling leaf brown when she walks

Closest bush to the road brown
fry bread smell in the grease brown

Horses graze as needles stitching the grass
She covers herself with porcupine quills,
raccoon stripes, feathers of the mottled hens
& skunk grass

Not awake yet brown in the head
of her buckskin dress
lonesome red of the plucked rooster comb

The metallic strip of silo
reminds her of a beading needle

Not muzzled with buttons
her bosom waddles under the duststorm
of her buckskin dress
somewhere
the prickly pear of her nippled flesh

She is the only squaw with a closet in her teepee

The first morning light
through the flat trees brown

Silver scissored as the river
she cuts through fields & hunting grounds
her brown buckskin dress fringed with elk teeth

She is on her way to the yard goods store
mouth stained red as winterberry

Gourd rattle brown, buckbrush brown,
wild turkey, wood duck brown,
running dog into the hills brown

Her brave hunts all season for pelts & hides
while she sits warm as campfire
like a yellow veined leaf

Leggins, sashes, belts, turtle shells, blankets,
shawls, combs, bags, hornet nest hats—

It takes a two-horse travois to get her
to winter camp.

Snore

You tell me I snore,
not even on my side of the bed
but next to you
like a plow against a tree.
I dream in a pink sundress —
a picket fence,
fragrant garden for corn & beans,
mouth open to sky
tiller motor running.

Right Justly

When he movd into the house
he wanted us to stomp & pray
out the evil spirits
  just in case they'd be there.

How cld they
when a medicine woman lived on the place
& left it to the church when she went to happier
grounds?

But a truck hauling brush
turnd on the road
  & he jumped up screaming—
deer prowler
  at the antlered beast.

We danced out the spirits
he carried on the place.
   How now pow wow
he jumps in the sow-yard with the bow-
    wow cow.

We passed the spirits to chickens
to peck their legs—
Eeeeevil spirits pock-marked
  as the dartboard.

W/ marbles shooting rabbit eyes
we stompd wild fires he once built in his head,
   still haunted him
as though evil spirits could open
a medicine woman's door, —
  climb in her unpainted windows,
crawl through yellowed wallpaper armoured w/
    prayer-chants.

We whooped & hawed until he sd nuf.
  The house
barricaded from deer prowlers
   from under his headband.

Barnyard

We have to have nice smiles
the mother says
her voice like a butcher knife in my head.

How living twenty years with a man who burned
away my limbs
rage grinned in me and you can still see the smile
nice as those on charred heads

lips pulled back
laughing like a mule.

Arrival of the Child

I travel north through Oklahoma
& Kansas to visit
her again.

A sack blows across the highway,
sticks to the front of the car.
Its tattered edge flaps like the wing of a bird
I once caught in the grill.

The car overheats anyway.
I slow & the sack falls off.

Why are we singled out?

I would struggle away but she pulls me back,
wobbly as the car in prairie wind.

She is waiting when I arrive in Missouri.
She says my name is on the back of an antique plate.

We look at her albums again,
a letter from Osceola when my brother was at camp,
find a transfer from the trolley
we once took to town.

Later I wash her back
& she sticks her swollen limb up for the sock—
moaning to the tumor
she carries in her side like a child.

One Age in a Dream

In this small town
the long last of it

this utter warning is not part of our inheritance

we should know better
we should bow and sing
this new birth

instead of filling it with tantrums and sobs
much like a climax
the wild asking
the contorted face

and my voice not strong anyway
tatters like a diaper

The glare of day pulls you back into itself
where you unbutton
your buttons
one by one
sagging and damp as the other end of a child

One after another
the guilts will let go—
Bump against them
drawn up tightly as a string
at the mouth of a gunny sack.

Genesis

Right here is where we came out of the ground,
stood straight up and took a sapling,
bent it for a house.

Even the shed on one leg
had more of a chance than we who married.

The slash of fencepost we put up
never reached the fields between us.

But we got it over with,
the meals and all the days working
and returning to the emptiness.
Each looking out the other way.

No, the early fields I return to
hold the husk of some wife I hardly remember.
The new one waits for fulfillment now
carrying the seed in her
while I am left with these divisions
whith I mend like an old quilt
or an oil slick
smeared with probability.

Dog

This dog has too many fleas he scratches
daily the nest of them in his fur then licks
      the scratches.
His dog eye looks at me. His nose sniffs the air.
He sighs when they are quiet
& snoozes in the sun.
But soon the flea glee heats the savage tribe of cannibals—

The raspy sound of scratching—
the dying breath of a parent
or ancestors rubbing sticks over open fire?
      How many does he think march to his rinky tune?

Garage

This can be counted on:
the garage mechanic, his dark
shelves,
batteries, tires,
stacks of oil cans & loops
of belts
hoopsnaked on the wall.

What is in the sparkling dark
that turns light in the cave
of the mechanic's garage?

The great backyard opens the ravages
of imagination.
The crowd of city houses,
the little garages up the alley
like batteries on the terraced shelves.

In the door I see
the car, open mouthed,
as though it were a dentist's office —
the garage mechanic leaning over the motor.
I see him under the light
regretting the erosion of battery,
the cavity
in that brown rootless tooth.
The trip to the zoo with the children
to see the rhino with stepping-stone teeth.

No less the island of the carburetor,
the dark human grease
the python squeezes
with his lovely spots.

When the car closes its mouth
in this cave,
this island of funnels, filters & dirt,

the mechanic wipes his hands
on the soiled rag.
I see him walk toward me and smile.
Ah, this is what it is about,
the squealing & writhing,
the agonies & narrow-necked garage
from which we finally emerge
alive.

Navajo

The bleating hill
fits your sheep

your headband
half-tied
    to the other

a rest you can't tend

This land
in the shadowed hole
    of your eye

let the father know
if you ever want

These graves before us
O-Sah-Ke-Pah
Ne-Shah-E
Emma Strikeaxe No Ear
Hum-Pah-To-Kah
marbles in the cement cross

The medicine woman
says your ear stops up
because you were near
    the dead

but pshnn-no
at Osage cemetery, Pawhuska,
these dead are gifts
for their having lived
in the glades of our mind

Our breasts tender
for grazing them
    Little Bear
Big Horse who went to war

A child's toy whistle I hear

the cat with a sound
of a diesel tractor
    on a hill
artillery fire
from Big Horse in war

I feel them moving
    like distant traffic
on the highway
descending
    climbing

in the glare
of this last summer heat
we are in the midst
of a freeway
bugs & birds
and spirits with bundles
    & lambs on their back

bleating
letting the father know
when they need a hand.

One Age in a Dream

They Gave Us the Umbrella

*—for the warrior who lamented that his horse
and gun were brought by the white man.*

In dreams
our flames rise from clouds
the buffalo snorting dust
hundreds & thousands of them on the prairie again
hard hat like old head dress
warrior with a hub cap face
a ke ya
punk a nu nu
mohawk haircut
then the man passes with a cross
& we're stomp dancing to the millennial hunting grounds
ancestors wait
where a squaw with turtle pot
bundle of twigs
blanket woven with signs
lights the evening fire
pure price of the trail
losing earth
for the blood of Christ
on hide drawings
our trails through the resin of trees
sap oozing like blood
like dreams from our heads
blown in two
where it goes
we go
protected under rain
the flat faith of it
Indian at the banjo
with a spatula they lifted us from the land
but look into the tinfoil
glittering ages joined in the everlasting repair shop
the welder's helmet
goggles

oh, our wounds closed up
& the scab of them peeled off
the glorious noise
of all who have lived the strain of fusion
our toenails trimmed
our voices waxed
& shouting
hosanna!

One Age in a Dream is Diane Glancy's second full length book of poetry. She is also the author of several chapbooks and an autobiography, *Two Dresses*, which appears in a volume of twelve Indian writers called *I Tell You Now*, published in 1986 by the Cooper Union and the University of Nebraska Press.

Diane Glancy is Artist-in-Residence for the State Arts Councils of Oklahoma and Arkansas. She is Poet-in-the-Schools for the Arts & Humanities Council of Tulsa, and Writer-in-Residence at the Heller Theater. She is the winner of the $1,000 playwriting prize from the Five Civilized Tribes, and was the 1984–1986 Laureate. Ms. Glancy is of Cherokee heritage and her work is included in several recent anthologies, including *Songs from this Earth on Turtle's Back* (Greenfield Review), *A Nation Within* (Outrigger Publishers, New Zealand), *The Clouds Threw this Light* (Institute of American Indian Arts Press), *A Gathering of Spirit* (Sinister Wisdom), and *These Hearts, These Poems* (Pueblo of Acoma Press).